Brave Tony

by Dennis Fertig
illustrated by Siri Weber Feeney

Core Decodable 112

McGraw Hill Education

Bothell, WA • Chicago, IL • Columbus, OH • New York, NY

MHEonline.com

Send all inquiries to:
McGraw-Hill Education
8787 Orion Place
Columbus, OH 43240

ISBN: 978-0-02-140686-9
MHID: 0-02-140686-3

Printed in Canada.

9 10 11 12 KOD 24

A Bright Light

On a hot night, Tony liked his window and blinds open. Then he could feel cool breezes. He could see the moon.

Lately, a bright light changed things. It filled Tony's room. He had to shut his blinds. The light came from the next house.

The house was Mr. Bloom's. He was new on the block. He did not talk much. He just stood and looked at plants.

Now Tony was not thinking about Mr. Bloom. Tony was reading a good book. It was about a brave man.

The man took a chance. He climbed the highest peak on Earth. The man was brave, but not foolish. He made good plans.

The book was true. The man was real. Tony liked true books. He liked them better than made-up books.

Soon Tony flipped his lamp switch. He had to go to sleep.

It was hot. Tony opened his blinds and window.

When he did, Tony's room was bright. It seemed like his lamp was still on. Tony shook his head. It was too bright!

A Good Plan

Tony knew what he had to do. He had to talk to Mr. Bloom soon. But Tony felt afraid.

Tony thought about how the brave man climbed the peak. That man made a good plan. Tony would, too.

The next afternoon, Tony went to Mr. Bloom. Tony carried the book with him. It helped him act bravely.

"Hi, Tony," said Mr. Bloom.

"Hi, Mr. Bloom," said Tony. Then Tony followed his plan. He told Mr. Bloom about the light.

Tony told him in a nice way. Mr. Bloom smiled and said, "Tony, you are right. I will turn down that light."

Mr. Bloom saw Tony's book. "I like that brave climber," he said.

He and Tony talked and talked. Brave Tony made a good pal.